Surprising Things Inmates Have Said

How education has failed America's youth.

A. Ruben

Printed in the United States of America.

Surprising Things Inmates Have Said: How education has failed America's youth / Ruben

ISBN: 978-0-9754590-5-8

Ickynicks Publishing

Front Cover by Adam Zillins

Note to the Reader

The following quotes by inmates of a correctional classroom are as humorous as they are tragic, revealing an appalling level of illiteracy and stressing even greater the value of education in today's youth; to hear an inmate reject the fact that the world is round is simply shocking, and yet that's only the beginning. Whether it's fearing that the Moon is crashing or that putting a crack in a globe means a crack in the world the staggering things inmates say and do is as shocking as it is scary when realizing just how many will return to society uneducated, unaware, and unable to critically think about problems they may face, including the consequences of poor decisions.

As incarcerated individuals, inmates are enrolled into a General Education Development course (G.E.D. or GED) with the intent to reduce recidivism, or repeat offending. After all, a GED does open more doors for work and the more opportunities an inmate has the greater the hope that he will succeed. At this book's facility, inmates receive a variety of programming including financial management, personal growth, drug abuse awareness and domestic violence. Yet, as much as a GED opens doors it is something that is earned, not given. Thus begins for many a journey of self-reliance and accountability; to earn one's GED is a matter of pride, a milestone, and for many the biggest achievement of their life. A few inmates have even cried tears of joy for just passing one out of the four tests.

This book's setting is a 90-day "boot camp" program, of which about 60 days are spent in the classroom. Thus, an inmate has limited time to earn his GED and must therefore be productive with his time.

Studying is something new to many, and received differently across the board. Some get into it. Others do not. Some need "street" metaphors to make sense of topics. Others just need a table and chair to sit at.

Even with the GED test switching over from paper to computer and the inherent challenges of that the resolve remains high for many inmates. Earning a GED is a formidable challenge, and for those that earn it comes a sense of pride, self-achievement, and even a sense of self worth. While the inmate thanks the teacher it is always the inmate who is told that earned it. The teacher was simply a guide.

This book captures the illiteracy not to mock but to draw attention to and raise awareness to the need of education in today's youth. While the quotes can be humorous the undertone is somber. The value of education can't be stressed enough. Often we go about our daily lives taking for granted the education of ourselves and those around us, whether in a bank talking to a teller, or at work, on the phone with a customer, or even shopping at a grocery store, but what is frightening is the illiteracy of these youth, incarcerated and uneducated.

While this book does speak on demographics (i.e. race and age) it is not the intention. The purpose of this book is to simply capture the sad truth and draw awareness to it, the need for change, and the indispensible value of teachers.

Acknowledgements

The author wishes to thank the following for their support, Lynn, Adam, Rochelle, Marilyn, Alex, and Sara. Thank you very much for your assistance in making this work possible.

The following are actual remarks and actions by incarcerated individuals.

For every student that asks why coming to school is so important. Here's why…

Recently, the new G.E.D. is computer based and is comprised of four tests, instead of five of the earlier paper model. These tests include content in the subject areas of Mathematics, Social Studies, Science, and Reading in Language Arts.

* * * * * * * * * * * *

1) After nearly 35 minutes an inmate finally gave up. He couldn't solve the problem that asked him to reduce 2/4. The answer was ½.

2) Several inmates were complaining that the room was too hot...they had pointed the fans towards the wall.

3) An inmate saw the moon during the day and thought it was crashing.

The Mathematics test includes knowledge of basic decimals, fractions, and percent's as well as algebra, geometry, inequalities and slopes on a graph.

* * * * * * * * * * *

4) An inmate asked the teacher if he had any kids. The teacher tried to evade the question by saying, "I don't know." To which the inmate replied without missing a beat, "Yeah, me too."

5) An inmate remarked that he must have done a practice test on the wrong side of the answer bubble sheet. He noted that the front side was the same as the backside. The teacher told him it was supposed to be like that.

The Social Studies portion of the test includes general knowledge of United States history as well as Civics & Government, including basic understanding of the Declaration of Independence, the US Constitution, the Civil War, the Cold War, and the three branches of government as well as the Electoral System.

* * * * * * * * * * * *

6) An inmate said aloud that he hoped to become "enough educated" to not get caught a second time.

7) Two inmates struggled to solve a math problem that asked them to solve for "x." Despite it being a multiple-choice question in which they could work backwards they had no idea.

8) An inmate was asked to solve the problem *8x - 4 when x = 3*. He asked what "when" meant.

The Science portion of the test emphasizes Life Science and Physical Science, including the anatomy of cells, reproduction and genes, chemical equations, atoms and magnetism.

* * * * * * * * * * *

9) An inmate was caught trying to steal a practice test answer sheet. He wanted to trade it for food. However, the answer sheet was open and available for anyone to check his work. So it actually had no value.

10) An inmate put "Biblical Hebrew" on his résumé as a foreign language.

11) "What language do they speak in Hawaii?"

The Reading in Language Arts section of the G.E.D. covers such topics as Main Ideas, Theme, Point-of-View, Cause & Effect, Compare & Contrast and Inferences. The test itself consists of three parts and is 2.5 hours long; this is the longest test of the four. Math is almost two hours long, and Science and Social Studies are 1.5 hours long.

* * * * * * * * * * * *

12) An inmate said he wasn't in class because he burned himself on the dishwasher while on kitchen duty. He said Medical's suggestion was for him to not keep putting his hand in the dishwasher.

13) When asked what the first thing an inmate would do when he got out was he answered, "Get some."

14) "Who's Benjamin Franklin?"

15) Dialogue between an inmate and the teacher:

I: "Do you have a car?"

T: "No, I walked here."

I: "What kind of car? Is it old, like a classic car?"

T: "No."

I: "If you had an old car, what would it be?"

T: "A model T."

I: "Is that an old car?"

T: "Yes."

I: "Would you get anything older than that?"

T: "A horse."

I: "What kind of horse?"

T: "One that moves."

Examinees of the G.E.D. must pass each subject with a score of 145 points out of 200. Passing with 175 points or better is considered honors, and some college institutions will count that towards credit.

* * * * * * * * * * *

16) An inmate apparently didn't know where countries were on a map. After several minutes of studying the map he found France and Germany, but struggled to find Poland.

17) An inmate was asked to point to Europe. He stared at it for a few minutes and then gave up. He said he didn't know which color it was.

18) "My answer wasn't wrong," said one inmate. "Just different than yours."

Inmates are usually started on the Social Studies or Science tests of the G.E.D. since those questions will later help an inmate on the Reading in Language Arts. The Science test for example, also has two writing prompts that will later help inmates on the Reading test.

* * * * * * * * * * *

19) When asked to find United Kingdom on a map an inmate thought it was two separate places. "I see kingdom, but united is above it."

20) Of all the countries in Europe to find, Great Britain is apparently the hardest.

21) When asked where the capital of the USA was the inmate replied, "It's on the west coast!"

22) Teacher trying to help an inmate find the US on a map.

T: "Where's Mexico."

1st Inmate: "I don't know."

2nd Inmate: "Sure you do. It's where you go when you break the law."

23) **1st Inmate:** "I'm a vegetarian. I don't eat beets."

2nd Inmate: "You mean beef. Beets are a vegetable."

1st inmate: "Oh snap! For real?"

The math portion of the G.E.D. is typically the most challenging and is therefore often reserved for last. Algebra polynomials are often one of the most difficult as examinees must incorporate basic skills such as addition, subtraction, multiplication and division as well as be aware of when the question requires solving or just simplifying. The order of operations is what consistently gets inmates.

* * * * * * * * * * *

24) An inmate neither knew why the American Revolution was fought or who it was against, but after a minute he was definitely sure it was China.

25) After finding Egypt and Iraq, an inmate struggled to find Syria. After several minutes of searching he finally gave up and insisted the teacher was "messing with him." He thought it was fictitious.

At this book's facility, resources can be limited for a variety of reasons, such as the Internet. Therefore, specific test-taking strategies have to be adapted, such as packets, worksheets, and simplified explanations to make sense of complex topics.

* * * * * * * * * * *

26) An inmate asked when New Mexico left Mexico?

27) An inmate was asked to find the USA on the map. He started in Africa.

28) An inmate thought that North on a map meant down. Even after being corrected, he still looked downwards.

With a limited number of computers at this book's facility and Internet prohibited, inmates in this setting have to prepare with book material. Additionally, test-taking strategies are just as important as building up stamina for test taking.

* * * * * * * * * * *

29) An inmate was looking at a world map on the wall. When asked if the fastest route to Australia was from Los Angeles or over Africa, he replied, "Well you have to go over Africa, because the map ends."

30) Another inmate was looking at the world map on the wall and when asked to find Alaska and Russia he remarked, "How 'bout that. They're really far apart!"

Inmates of this book's setting are typically doubtful of their abilities and talents, taking the teacher's strategies with a grain of salt until passing their exams. After each passing score, inmates love to throw out a holler of celebration.

* * * * * * * * * * *

31) Later on, another inmate was also asked to find the US. After staring at it for a while he decided that "USA" and the "United States of America" were not the same thing and moved on.

32) An inmate was asked to find the capital of the United States. After a few minutes of looking in the southwest he was hinted to look on the east side. "Oh snap, that's where I'm from," he said.

In this book's classroom setting, the typical demographics are 50% African-American, 50% White, and on occasion 5% Hispanic or Native American. However, race has little impact upon one's determination to succeed.

* * * * * * * * * * *

33) An inmate looked puzzled when he was told that cars and trains didn't exist at the time of the American Revolution. He thought we should have just rolled the British over with tanks.

34) An inmate couldn't pronounce Babylonians. So he said Baby Lions.

35) An inmate insisted that the capital of the US was in the Midwest. When asked to explain, he tilted the globe.

The classroom within this book is at a "boot-camp" facility meaning inmates are drilled during the day and attend G.E.D. class at night. Other courses are also held, including work-readiness, life management and substance abuse.

* * * * * * * * * * *

36) Apparently, Hawaii is easily mistaken for being Mexico.

37) An inmate found India, but struggled to find the Indian Ocean. He was looking for it in North America.

38) An inmate neither knew what the US Constitution was nor the Declaration of Independence, so when told there was a Bill of Rights, he replied, "Oh snap, for real?"

As G.E.D. class is held in the evening at this book's facility, many inmates are already exhausted from a full day of exercise, work detail, and other courses. Consequently, this makes it all the more challenging for inmates to focus. Thus, it becomes an issue of self-motivation as well as teacher strategies to achieve the end goal.

* * * * * * * * * * * *

39) An inmate asked if former US President John Quincy Adams was a woman.

40) An inmate was shown an antique-looking replica of the Declaration of Independence. He asked if it was the original. When told it was not, he asked if the original was in the school office and if the teacher had just used the copier.

Younger inmates, aging between 18-21, are required by state law to attend three hours a day of G.E.D. class. Older inmates are only given an hour, but can be granted a second. In this book's classroom, the second hour is issued as a privilege based on strong effort and determination. Any goofing off, idle chitchat, or misbehavior results in the loss of that privilege.

* * * * * * * * * * *

41) An inmate was staring at Russia and Alaska on the world map and said, "Huh, I guess the world is kind of round!"

42) An inmate was asked to identify a major city on the East Coast. He answered Canada.

43) When asked to name a Civil Rights leader the inmate answered Kim Jong-un, the leader of North Korea.

44) Inmate logic never ceases to be amazing.
1st Inmate to Teacher: "Why do I need to study? I was the top student in my algebra class in school."
2nd Inmate to 1st: "So why are you in here then?"

45) Two inmates were talking about social studies:
1st Inmate: "The Cold War is a lot like me and the police, 'cause we always be seeing a lot of each other."
2nd Inmate: "No, that's not what a cold war is."
1st Inmate: "Well, then this shit just got real."

As a "boot-camp" facility, inmates are released back into society after 90 days, pending completion of the program. If terminated, however, inmates return to prison or jail. After the first month, inmates are placed in a G.E.D. class, giving them only about 60 days to earn it.

* * * * * * * * * * *

46) "Who's Darwin?"

47) An inmate saw the teacher grading his work. "You writing in black n' white," he asked. The teacher said, "You mean pencil?"

48) "Man, I know stuff," said one inmate, who couldn't find his own state on a map.

49) "I'm too ghetto to learn," said one inmate, trying to excuse himself from studying.

It could be said that part of teaching is helping students discover their talents and boosting their self-confidence. Some teachers at this book's facility publicly post the earners of a G.E.D. Some teachers however do not. An inmate asked one teacher why he did not post them. The teacher replied, "Did the world help you earn your G.E.D., or was it you?"

* * * * * * * * * * *

50) An inmate encouraged another to cheat right in front of the teacher's desk. Apparently, some lessons remain unlearned.

51) An inmate asked the teacher if there was a pill he could take to become smarter.

52) An inmate asked the teacher if he had also gone through prison to get his G.E.D. too.

53) Conversation between a teacher and an inmate.
T: "So how did you know the answer was C?"
I: "Because that's the answer in the back of the book!"

54) The worldview of inmates is often very narrow. Much of what they know comes from books or TV.
1st Inmate: "Hot things turn to snow in winter."
2nd inmate: "No they don't. They turn cold and freeze like a waterfall."
1st Inmate: "Shows what you know! Waterfalls don't freeze, because they're just pictures."

Although this book isn't focused on demographic statistics, it is noteworthy to mention that in this book's setting age played as much of a factor as other variables. From purely observation, the most revealing difference of studious behavior is between the ages of 22 and 23. The older an inmate is the more studious he is.

* * * * * * * * * * *

55) An inmate kindly informed the teacher that the peanut butter and jelly sandwich couldn't have been invented without "the Black man."

56) An inmate struggling in a subject matter confessed he should have stayed in school. He was learning how to read.

57) "Dr. Seuss taught me all about trees."

The classroom setting within this book is a white-painted concrete wall, tiled floor, a drop ceiling, tables and chairs and a window. There are educational posters on the wall as well as motivational phrases. The teacher's desk is manufactured from the state's furniture shop.

* * * * * * * * * * *

58) After having read about the American Revolution, an inmate was quizzed on who wrote the Declaration of Independence and why. He answered, "England, 'cause they didn't like France."

59) An inmate admitted he knew chemistry very well since he used to have a periodic table above his meth lab.

60) "I wasn't wrong. I was just a letter off."

With approximately only 60 days to earn a G.E.D. time plays a major factor in this book's classroom. Thus in addition to an inmate's personal motivation, teachers also have to develop a strategic game plan to help inmates pass as many exams as possible.

* * * * * * * * * * *

61) When asked to define the Cold War, an inmate replied, "Well sometimes you just gotta give a-bombs to your neighbors. The world's a strange place."

62) The question asked what the conclusion was from the reading passage. So, the inmate asked where he could find the clue in the passage? (conCLUEsion)

63) "What page is 15 on?"

The Reading, Social Studies and Science portions of the test can each be achieved in as little as 2-3 weeks. The Math portion of the G.E.D. however requires between 3-5 weeks of preparation. A major factor in achieving a G.E.D. is a student's willingness and effort.

* * * * * * * * * * *

64) The inmate left several answer bubbles blank. When told he should at least guess, he replied, "I did. I guessed that I didn't have to guess, so I left it blank."

65) An inmate didn't know who Malcolm X was, but he could name several rap artists.

66) "Did anybody ever miss their stop on the Underground Railroad?"

As the evening G.E.D. courses only allow for part-time employment, many teachers at this book's facility work in public schools or at community adult education facilities. Some are retired and do this to continue their love of education. Many are also parents, coaches, mentors, and volunteers in their community.

* * * * * * * * * * * *

67) Another inmate knew who Martin Luther King Jr. was, just not who the civil rights leader had represented. The inmate was African-American.

68) "What does Supply and Demand have to do with economics?"

69) An inmate was confused about shoppers lining up to buy things the day after Thanksgiving. He thought people only lined up to be counted.

As part of working in a prison, overfamiliarity with inmates is cautioned against, particularly because teachers often have a big heart. Overfamiliarity can be defined as becoming too friendly. Therefore, teachers at this book's facility were referred to as the first letter of their last name. So, Mr. Smith became Mr. S.

* * * * * * * * * * *

70) When asked what branch of government the Senate was in the inmate said, "The USA, no wait, Russia."

71) An inmate was reading a book on cars instead of studying. When asked how he expected to earn his G.E.D. without studying, he replied, "I just take each day, one at a time."

72) An inmate to the teacher. "Geez, now why'd you go and put a spark in me. Now I want to learn."

Before it was removed, the writing prompt (or extended response) of the Social Studies portion of the G.E.D. was arguably one of the most challenging parts of the test. In preparation, inmates in this book's classroom were trained on three levels of difficulty, using Abraham Lincoln's Gettysburg Address as the final level. Inmates had to compare Lincoln's address to a critical review written by a newspaper published shortly thereafter. Inmates had to argue which source better explained why so many died at the Battle of Gettysburg.

* * * * * * * * * * * *

73) An inmate tried to hide a pair of contraband scissors. Unfortunately, the teacher's desk probably wasn't the best hiding spot.

74) An inmate was told to stand up in class after falling asleep too many times. So, he slept while holding his book.

75) An inmate couldn't find Florida, but found Cuba.

Of the Science writing prompts, one of the most difficult for inmates is creating an experiment. Being able to think about a step-by-step process is certainly much harder than filling in a bubble.

* * * * * * * * * * *

76) An inmate complained that the room was too cold, and yet he continued to sit next to the cold window.

77) The inmate asked the teacher if he had brought in a laptop or cell phone. Obviously not, but that didn't stop him from asking.

78) "What's this word?" an inmate asked. The word was Jerusalem. He'd never heard of it.

79) Rising standards is easier said than done:
Teacher to inmate: "I expect that lesson to be done by the end of the hour."
I: "When will that be?"
T: "At the end of the hour."
I: "I thought you meant when this class ends."
T: "This class ends at the end of the hour."

80) An inmate with poor grammar claimed he didn't need a GED.
Inmate: "Where I'm from I'm king."
Teacher: "You mean *a* king."
I: "That's what I said."

Within the Reading through Language Arts portion of the exam, one of the most challenging content areas for inmates is inferring. Being able to infer what is happening in a literary piece is remarkably difficult, because it requires thinking critically. Nevertheless, it helps to ask an inmate what he can infer about the temperature if it is snowing.

* * * * * * * * * * * *

81) A new, talkative inmate to class noticed how quiet it was and how everyone was studying. "Is it gonna be like this all the time?" he asked. An older inmate replied, "Brains be drivin' here."

82) An inmate was looking at the copy of the Declaration of Independence. When he saw the date of July 4th he said, "Hey, that's Independence Day! I thought we did fireworks 'cause of that movie!"

There are approximately 15-20 inmates in a G.E.D. classroom. One of the most common questions people often ask a corrections teacher is about security. Does he or she feel endangered? The answer is that most inmates at this book's facility want to go home. They only have 90 days, and it's either get through the boot camp discipline or go back to prison. Also, most- if not all- inmates regard a teacher as someone trying to help.

* * * * * * * * * * *

83) One inmate was overhead telling another about his plans after getting out. He said, "I'm gettin' back to the money's."

84) "Is the Pope the head of the Pope Church?"

85) "Are there any humans in Rome?"

86) An inmate was surprised to learn about WWII. "It's a lot like Call of Duty!"

Each teacher designs his or her lessons differently to make the most of the 60 days available. While the math exam is often reserved for last, some teachers will nevertheless incorporate math lessons as inmate's progress through the other subject matters. Mean, median and mode is an example of one that happens to overlap into multiple content areas.

* * * * * * * * * * *

87) An inmate asked if all the presidents had signed the Declaration of Independence, including President Obama.

88) An inmate was told the Declaration of Independence is in Washington D.C. "Man, that's gonna cost some chicken to get there," he said, referring to money. An older inmate overhead that. "Man, I eat it. I ain't calling my money that also!"

What is perhaps most fascinating about teaching an inmate is the moment of epiphany that he has when he learns the meaning of a particular word or phrase. In one instance, an inmate found that another synonym for independence was freedom. Suddenly, he had a whole new regard for the Declaration of Independence.

* * * * * * * * * * *

89) An inmate asked if the Mona Lisa painting was a man.

90) "Didn't World War II happen like 3 years ago?"

91) "The Civil War happened like six years after the American Revolution, right?"

92) It took 3 inmates to find Los Angeles, CA on the world map.

93) An inmate was asked to find the Panama Canal:

I: "Where's that?"

T: "In Panama."

I: "Where's Panama?"

T: "In Central America."

I: "Where's that?"

T: "Between North and South America."

I: "Shit if I know where those two are!"

T: "You're in North America."

For many in this book's classroom, the G.E.D. opens doors to many more opportunities in life, from better pay to a ladder that can be climbed. There are those who realize this early on and those who do not. Then there are the exceptions... one inmate came to prison to earn his GED, because he said that's where his dad and brother got theirs.

* * * * * * * * * * *

94) An inmate was studying the world map on the wall. When asked what he was looking for he replied, "Atlantis."

95) An inmate asked the teacher why he had to ask for permission to enter the classroom. He wanted to just come right in. So, the teacher asked him if he would enter someone's home without permission. "Uh, yeah," he replied.

96) Two inmates were talking about what they'd do when they got out. One said he was going to go on a cruise in the Caribbean.

1st Inmate: "I can leave the country. I'm just on probation, not parole."

2nd Inmate: "No you can't. You have to meet with your probation officer."

1st Inmate: "Sure I can. I just have to be back in time."

Despite low education levels, many inmates in this book's classroom pick up concepts quickly. Unfortunately, a major hindrance to earning a G.E.D. is their lack of focus, which comes from being easily distracted by talking with others. To counter that, classroom management is paramount.

* * * * * * * * * * *

97) An inmate was shocked to learn people leave tips at restaurants that don't have drive-thru windows.

98) An inmate was asked which was the shorter route on the world map on the wall, from Alaska to Japan or from the United Kingdom to Japan. He answered the latter, because, "the UK is closer to it on the map."

99) An inmate thought stick shift was for time travel.

An inmate once celebrated that he had received a score of 148 on his test. At the time, passing was 150. Despite failing, he nevertheless felt it was a major accomplishment. After all, as he said it was the closest he had ever come to something meaningful in his life.

* * * * * * * * * * * *

100) An inmate was complaining about how unsavory the food was as well as how much the officers got in his face. Another inmate replied, "Well, if you don't like the food or service then don't come back to the gray bar hotel!"

101) An African-American inmate sarcastically answered a corrections officer, "Yes, boss-man." The officer was African-American.

Inmates are encouraged to use a Dictionary and Thesaurus to help them with big words. Both resources are often new to an inmate, but both become very popular as inmates begin to see the advantages of looking up words... including legal words.

* * * * * * * * * * * *

102) An inmate asked about 401K's and investing. After a brief explanation on compound interest the inmate replied, "Well shit, I'll make that in a weekend!"

103) An inmate was boasting how much money he made selling drugs. "And you know where that got me?" he asked. Another inmate answered for him, "Here, dumbass!"

104) "Does capitalism mean kidnapping?"

At this facility, teachers create a test list every week, naming inmates who have demonstrated strong proficiency in a subject matter. The first test is critical, because those that pass suddenly develop intrinsic motivation to study.

* * * * * * * * * * *

105) An inmate asked the teacher if he was a college professor. "Wait, disregard that question," he said, and then asked the very same question again. "So, are you a professor or something?"

106) An inmate was early to class and was told to come back next hour. "When will that be?" he asked.

107) "Who do I talk to about changing the weather?"

Sometimes a teacher has to find a way to relate subject matter in a way that an inmate can understand. In one instance, an inmate finally understood why the Japanese bombed Pearl Harbor after a teacher over-simplified it using a street reference. "If you're a buyer on a street and you go beat up another buyer and the seller cuts you off, then what are you going to do about it?" The inmate replied, "I'd retaliate."

* * * * * * * * * * * *

108) An inmate told the teacher he had PTSD, because studying gave him stress.

109) An inmate said he was going to college to get a PHDH. The teacher asked if he meant PhD. "Yeah," he said, "but I'm putting an 'H' on mine 'cause that's what's up."

110) An inmate asked where the border of a country was?

Another instance of helping relate subject matter to inmates is with the Cold War. The inmate finally understood after the teacher explained the superpower struggle by saying it was like a turf war on a global scale. By over-simplifying it as gangs trying to control a street the inmate was finally able to understand.

* * * * * * * * * * *

111) "Calculators give you answers," said an inmate with an astonished look on his face.

112) An inmate was mocking at how easy math inequalities and functions were to another inmate. He was later caught cheating.

113) "I guess Lincoln was kinda smart 'cause he wrote the Gettysburg Address. I guess he got a G.E.D."

Some light-hearted euphemisms when referring to the prison school have been, "It's an all boy's school," or "It's a school of hard knocks," or "It's the largest school in the state," or even, "There's always a captive audience."

* * * * * * * * * * *

114) "Help, I'm being held prisoner!" wrote an inmate on his class folder.

115) An inmate was not tech-savvy, because when asked to put the computer mouse at the top of the screen he did exactly just that.

116) An inmate didn't know the difference between a fact and an opinion. He argued that his crime was just the judge's opinion.

117) Racism and bigotry takes on a rather ironic dynamic in prison. An African-American complained how he felt like he was being treated like a "Hebrew slave" as a prisoner and that his White teacher couldn't relate to him and his struggle. Little did he realize the teacher was in fact Jewish.

118) Again, racism is rather humorously slanted in prison. An African-American inmate was talking about how "the system" was racist and how the government owed him compensation for having "supported" slavery. When the teacher asked if any other groups had been compensated for their struggles the inmate replied, "Yeah, the Indians!" The teacher asked, "You mean the Native Americans?" "Same difference."

119) In continuing the slavery discussion, the teacher asked if any others had been compensated. An inmate said, "Yeah, the Jews, cause now they own the world!" The teacher asked whether that was more about personal perseverance rather than reparations. "They're Jews, man," he replied, "They don't need a handout!"

120) The "debate" over slavery
and compensation came to
an abrupt end when the
teacher challenged the
spokesman-inmate who
was taking a lead role in the
conversation to think like a
businessman in terms of
economics. If his labor cost
was $0 and slaves were
cheap to buy would he then
treat them well or not,
especially when he was
making such huge profits?
The African-American
inmate hesitated at first.
The he answered
unashamedly, "Shit, I'm
rolling in my money's ain't
I? Fuck em."

With the elimination of the Social Studies writing portion on the GED exam many inmates at this facility were able to use the additional time to focus on evidence-based questions, which further improved scores.

* * * * * * * * * * *

121) Another inmate also struggled with fact v. opinion. So when the teacher pointed to the white-painted wall to illustrate what a fact was the inmate said, "Yeah, maybe it's white, but who knows for sure."

122) As the weather got cooler, many inmates complained that they were getting cold. So to warm up they just started farting.

123) **Inmate**: "I guess being in prison makes me a criminal."
Teacher: "I'm teaching a class in a prison. Does that make me a criminal?"
I: "I don't know, maybe. What did you do to get in?"

124) **1st Inmate**: "I got swag."
2nd Inmate: "You know that that term used to mean you were gay."
1st Inmate: "I ain't got no swag."

The tragedy of a lack of education was perhaps most vivid during one instance when an inmate was told the stars in the night sky were actually suns, and that the universe has billions of stars. He thought the night sky just simply lit up.

* * * * * * * * * * *

125) "What's an author?"

126) Dominant and recessive genes were being explained to an inmate. Unfortunately, he wasn't fully grasping it. When asked what it might mean if he and his "baby mama" had brown eyes but their child had blue eyes he got upset. "Well then, it ain't mine is it?"

127) It took five inmates to find Mali on the world map.

There are moments of revelation between inmates that are worth noting. In one instance, two inmates were debating about the merits of the facility. One argued that it was a worthless place and did nothing but harass him. The other replied, "No man, you don't get it. It's not about what they give you. It's about what you take out of here."

* * * * * * * * * * *

128) An inmate was caught doodling instead of studying. He had drawn a house with a dog leash in the yard, but no dog, a garage with no car, and a public trash receptacle commonly seen along streets beside a barbecue grill.

129) "Do deer live in trees?"

130) "Do we speak British?"

Another moment of revelation was one inmate who said he wasn't addicted to meth; he was just addicted to the process of making it. Without missing a beat, another inmate said, "Just keep telling yourself that."

* * * * * * * * * * *

131) The question was about velocity and momentum. It was describing two cars on a collision course, and when asked what the best way to slow the velocity the inmate replied, "Jump."

132) After trying to explain the question a bit better the inmate said to the teacher, "I thought we were doing a science problem, not real world stuff!"

133) When asked what DNA was the inmate replied, "Do Not Ask."

A final moment of revelation was when an inmate in his early 30's told one in his early 20's to study and take advantage of the teachers. The younger one figured he could just get back into high school. "And what if you can't," the older one said, challenging his way of thinking. "Get your life together now and get a G.E.D."

* * * * * * * * * * *

134) "Damn, Russia is big. That's a lot of orange."

135) "I bet Russia could easily be invaded. I bet nobody's tried that yet!"

136) "Do we own Alaska, or do I need a passport?"

137) "Hitler made me rich, 'cause he invented meth."

Sometimes there can be a waiting list for inmates to get into G.E.D. class. In this case, those with the strongest skill set in reading and math are selected first in hopes they can earn theirs quickly and teach the incoming new ones.

* * * * * * * * * * *

138) An inmate was told he had to wait 60 calendar days before retaking the exam again. He was also about to leave prison. He replied, "Yeah, but that's in here. Do I have to wait out there?"

139) An inmate saw a deer at the window. "Hey, it's a horse! No wait, it ain't. Shit, you know what I mean."

140) An inmate asked how many days he had left before getting out if yesterday he had 21.

141) When showing an inmate
the antique copy of the
Declaration of
Independence another
suddenly burst from his
chair to see it, thinking the
teacher had the real one.
I: "Is that the real one?"
T: "No, it's a copy."
I: "That's got to be real."
T: "It's not. It's a copy."
I: "But it looks so old."
T: "It's a copy."
I: "But look at the paper."
T: "It's a copy."
I: "No way that's a fake."
T: "It's a copy."

Working in a prison classroom means not wearing certain articles of clothing, such as a tie. It is always a possible scenario that an inmate could attempt to strangle.

* * * * * * * * * * *

142) While reading a science story problem that talked about Copernicus, a 15th Century scientist, the inmate suddenly said, "Hey I know that dog! He's from that movie with that time-machine car."

143) Inmates often ask about current events in the world. When told there were tentative missions to Mars an inmate replied, "Yeah, but how are we going to get oxygen there?"

Part of working in a prison classroom also means security is paramount. Recent technology allows teachers to wear a personal protection device that has GPS, so in the event of an emergency custody staff can find the teacher within two feet of his or her exact location. Previously, custody might run through the whole building.

* * * * * * * * * * *

144) When naming allied countries in WWII, inmates often choose Germany.

145) An inmate was late to G.E.D. class, because he opted to celebrate his job promotion rather than study. He had just been promoted to potato peeler.

146) Inmates often confuse Austria with Australia. "Let's put another shrimp on the Barbie," one said.

Another part of being a teacher in a prison is the security training. Typically alongside corrections officers, teachers are shown where and how to use pressure points, self-defense techniques, and can observe Taser scenarios.

* * * * * * * * * * *

147) An inmate once showed the teacher a record of every meal he had had at the facility. When asked why he had recorded them he said, "Why not? People record snowfalls."

148) An inmate had 30 days left before getting out. He didn't think he could get his G.E.D. in that time even though he had passed two tests already. When the teacher offered to put more resources at his disposal the inmate decided that it was just easier to quit.

Typically, whenever the Great Depression is discussed, an inmate will ask what Wall Street is. This leads into a brief discussion of investing, what stocks are, dividends and mutual funds. Most if not all are surprised to learn that they don't have to win the lottery to invest; the sense that their world has untapped doors overcomes any feeling of defeatism and inspires further learning.

* * * * * * * * * * * *

149) When asked what democracy was the inmate replied, "I don't know. What democrats do?"

150) "Can I get a job that requires a G.E.D. but just lie and say I have one?"

151) Are there Mexicans in Texas?" Which was quickly followed up by, "Wait a second, what makes New Mexicans more newer than Mexicans?"

When trying to remember the 3 branches of government, inmates use the first letter of each to form words they know. So Executive becomes Election, Judicial becomes Judge and Legislative becomes Law. The latter they remember because it's what they broke.

* * * * * * * * * * *

152) An inmate was troubled by something he had just heard. He asked if the world was really round. When the teacher pointed to the globe in the classroom he replied, "Yeah, but if that were really true then I'd always be dizzy."

153) An inmate thought the Cold War was just an intermission between the two world wars.

Of all the resources in the classroom the two interests of inmates are the dictionary and the world map. Inmates like to learn legal words and talk about places they want to go. While it's sad that many can't find the United States on a map let alone read a map, they nevertheless enjoy looking at it.

* * * * * * * * * * * *

154) A chatty inmate was told to get back to studying, and that a G.E.D. could help him in getting a better paying job. The inmate disagreed. "Man, I made three times what these guards make."

155) Suspecting the inmate had cheated, the teacher asked him to explain how he got his answer. "Man, it's like this. I read the paragraph and just like that it came to me. Ya feel me?"

The most crucial element of classroom management in a prison setting is respect. An inmate who disrespects a teacher that has clearly helped others earn their GED is immediately corrected by his fellow inmates, and often returns the next day with a much better attitude.

* * * * * * * * * * *

156) The inmate was asked which historical and important document contains information about the US government, including the Bill of Rights. The inmate replied, "The Ten Commandments."

157) An inmate wanted to find something more difficult on the world map on the wall. So the teacher asked him to find Rwanda. The inmate replied, "Okay, but what country does she live in?"

158) Inmate to teacher: "Should I take the orange pill to get better?"

T: "I'm not a doctor. Plus, I have no idea what orange pill you're talking about."

I: "You know, an orange pill. You peel it."

T: "Wait, what? An orange? Why don't you just eat the orange?"

I: "Oh yeah, good idea."

159) Several inmates wanted to leave class early to get a haircut, but the officer refused them asking instead if they were okay working minimum wage jobs the rest of their life.

Inmate: "But I don't need a GED. I was in sales before this. I'll just go back to that."

Officer: "Selling drugs doesn't count, stupid!"

Inmates may struggle with reading, even get annoyed when pushed to sound out a word or look it up in the dictionary, but most if not all appreciate the dedication of a teacher. One inmate smiled proudly with success after sounding out "Emancipation Proclamation." He then wanted to learn more about Abraham Lincoln and the Civil War.

* * * * * * * * * * *

160) An inmate insisted that Montana was on the West Coast. When told it wasn't because it didn't border the Pacific Ocean the inmate replied, "Yeah, but my neighbors live across the hall. Ain't he in the same apartment building as me? Montana ain't that far from the ocean."

161) After learning he had passed a GED test, an astounded inmate said, "My mom would be trip'n if she knew I was studying!"

Inmates enjoy competing in nearly everything whenever and however they can. The younger inmates like to compare demerits against each other like sports statistics: how many in a day and how severe the offense.

* * * * * * * * * * * *

162) Two inmates were overheard guessing what staff makes. Just as they were redirected back to their studies one said to the other, "Don't matter really what they make. Their chicken's legal."

163) An inmate said he knew his percent's, so when asked what 50% off at a store meant he replied sarcastically, "Uh, more money for when I sell it!"

Inmates also get a laugh getting each other into trouble. One inmate told another to show the teacher what "304" on a calculator spelled upside was. Neither the teacher nor the officer in the room was amused that it spelled "hoe."

* * * * * * * * * * * *

164) While quizzing an inmate on basic economics of supply & demand the teacher used the example of shoes like Nike. When asked who might demand the shoes from the market a second inmate burst out with what he thought was the answer. "Black people!" He was African-American.

165) An inmate thought the Tasmanian devil spun like in the cartoon. "Why else would he spin then?"

Veteran inmates in a classroom warn new inmates if the teacher is a stickler for the rules. Inmates refer to getting caught as being shot. "Careful, or you'll get shot." It can be amusing to other inmates when someone keeps getting shot for the same offense, such as using profanity.

* * * * * * * * * * *

166) During a brief lesson on the Solar System the inmate was told the Sun would eventually end in 5 billion years. He replied, "Guess I better get my GED soon then."

167) An inmate tried to pretend he was studying. As soon as the teacher looked over at him he said to another, "So the Declaration of Independence is the same as the Constitution?"

Learning can be as foreign to an inmate as technology. One inmate asked what the dot on the calculator was for unaware it was for decimals. Nevertheless, many absorb education like a sponge. One amazed inmate said, "School is for suckers, but I should have stayed in it."

* * * * * * * * * * *

168) Inmates are prohibited from cursing in the classroom, but to many it's second nature. Many don't realize it until they think about it. "Hell, I know I wasn't swearing. Ah shit. I mean sorry."

169) Explaining the Cold War often gets surprised looks, especially when trying to stress the threat of nuclear Armageddon. "I guess war is a bad thing," said one. "Good thing I'm in here."

Learning is a process, and so change doesn't happen overnight. Often an inmate will stumble many times, breaking the rules or reverting back to old habits before he allows himself to try new things.

* * * * * * * * * * *

170) On the subject of economics an inmate decided to be the spokesman for the class by saying that everyone who was in for selling drugs knew all about supply & demand. "Hell, we're all entrepreneurs."

171) An inmate apparently didn't know the difference between decrease and increase, because he had tried to ask for a decrease in his wage.

As part of the learning process, an inmate will try and bend the rules, manipulate staff, resist or lash out, curse and do whatever it takes to get removed from class, but against strong resilience from a teacher that believes in the potential of everyone it is only a matter of time.

* * * * * * * * * * *

172) There are educational posters in the classroom. An inmate asked if the teacher had ever been to a volcano. When the teacher said no, he replied, "I guess they don't let you out much then."

173) For whatever reason the answer choice "nuclear" is more often picked when answering what a flashlight is. The other choices are chemical, electrical and mechanical.

As part of the learning process, every teacher teaches differently. Some teachers will assess an inmate right away on an exam in order to see which types of questions he needs help on. Others will wait, devoting time to study until the inmate is ready to test. Though different, the goal remains the same: inmate success and reducing recidivism.

* * * * * * * * * * *

174) Inmates in school take an assessment exam. Typically this is done every quarter in order to assess any progress. There are four levels, Easy, Medium, Difficult, and Advanced. One inmate said aloud, "Guess I'm ahead 'cause E comes after A."

175) An inmate asked if the teacher had graduated from Kaplan Test Prep. "How else would you know so much about the textbook?"

One of the most impossible days to test an inmate is right before he is released. His mind is only on leaving. For some this is scary. For others this is a day long waited.

* * * * * * * * * * *

176) An inmate was asked to move after being disruptive. He was told to sit under a WWII poster. He hesitated. "That was a big war. I don't want to get hurt if I sit near it."

177) An inmate couldn't grasp that the world was round. "Russia is close to the US, but also so far away!"

178) The inmate got in trouble for vandalism. In the bathroom, he wrote, "Vandalism is wrong."

Anything can happen the day of a test, from bad news to being in the wrong spot at the wrong time. So no matter what degree of preparation an inmate has done beforehand the real test is whether he can stay focused.

* * * * * * * * * * *

179) Inmates don't always keep up with current events. One thought Saddam Hussein, the former leader of Iraq, was still in power. "Why was Iraq invaded?" he asked. "He should've been able to invade Kuwait. But I guess you get to do those kinds of things when you're the president."

180) An inmate didn't know anything about the confederate flag, except that it was in the Dukes of Hazard TV show. He was African-American.

The rules for testing in a prison are different than on the outside. Every inmate is patted down before he enters the room. He is told what he can and what he cannot bring into the testing room, and once inside he cannot leave to use the restroom. He must do so ahead of time or wait until after he is done. On occasion, an inmate will wet himself.

* * * * * * * * * * *

181) The directions asked to revise the sentence to correct the wording. The sentence read, "Trent's sister encouraged him to become a nurse, who is a medical professional." Instead of replacing the word, "who" for "which" the inmate simply added the word "big" before "sister."

Prior to entering the classroom, inmates file alongside the wall and ask to enter. This is protocol at the boot camp. An inmate must ask permission to enter.

* * * * * * * * * * *

182) As part of a science lesson, an inmate was asked to list animals in his environment. He said, "birds, bugs, and dinosaurs." He was insistent.

183) In trying to help inmates understand the gravity of the Cold War and the threat of nuclear war the teacher tried to compare the deadly use of nuclear bombs to the power of the ancient Egyptian chariot. "Chariot bombs," the inmate replied. "I love those fireworks!"

Whenever an inmate needs to use the restroom, or head as it is called at the boot camp, he must stand outside the classroom with a wooden pass. This pass has the room number on it. An inmate without a pass can be written up for being out of place.

* * * * * * * * * * *

184) Just as an aside, the teacher shared Einstein's theory of relativity. The inmate replied, "I feel ya, but I like things just the way they are."

185) During the summer, the sign on the window read, "Keep closed. Wasps come in." The inmate opened it to see.

186) "Where'd China go? Oh snap, you have to look on the other side of the map."

At this book's boot camp setting one of the fastest ways to be terminated from the program is by bringing in contraband. Many inmates work van detail, which is going into the community to clean public areas or assist at recycling centers. Trying to smuggle anything in, even a used cigarette, will result in immediate termination and the inmate will be sent back to jail or prison.

* * * * * * * * * * * *

187) An inmate was looking at the world map on the wall. "Why did each country pick their color?"

188) An inmate wished to share some shocking news. "Nicholas Cage is a real person? I thought he was an actor!"

189) Inmates receive demerits for wrongdoings, such as profanity. One inmate said, "I'm not cursing anymore. I get too many demerits for shit I didn't do."

In addition to contraband coming in, inmates will try and steal. While it isn't to say theft is a common crime the best policy is to watch one's belongings. A gate manifest not only limits what can be brought in, but also helps reduce personal loss from theft. Inmates have been known to steal teacher's lunches.

* * * * * * * * * * *

190) An inmate felt being called a convict by a corrections officer was derogatory and disrespectful. Never mind he had no remorse for his crime.

191) "I'm faithful to my girl," the inmate said, explaining his standards. "I just cheat with her friends."

192) An inmate told the teacher he had to stop learning, because his brain was working.

With theft in mind, every teacher has a cabinet that can be locked. An orderly classroom further limits thievery.

* * * * * * * * * * *

193) The inmate admitted ripping pages out of a book, which he wasn't supposed to do. He said that since someone else had already done it he figured then that it was okay for him to do it. So when the teacher asked him whether he thought breaking into a home that someone else had already broken into was also okay he replied, "I don't see why not. It's fair game then."

Through the process of learning, an inmate may resist, get into trouble, call the teacher names, and even try and start a fight, but this is nothing more than an inmate's test of the teacher. Persistence and perseverance as well as genuine interest in his growth will defeat the inmate's efforts.

* * * * * * * * * * *

194) An inmate accidently put a crack in the classroom globe and then quickly looked down at his feet to make sure he wasn't standing in it.

195) An African-American inmate heard that Harriet Tubman was replacing Andrew Jackson on the $20 bill. He remarked, "That's tripp'n, but what'd she do?"

Learning to succeed is often like a roller coaster. Many inmates will try, slip back into their old habits, and then repeat. The trick is to guide them off this cycle and entirely towards success. Unfortunately, it is not something that can be told or done for them. It is a journey they must take.

* * * * * * * * * * *

196) A Hispanic inmate looked puzzled during a history lesson about European colonization of the Americas. "You mean people from Spain also speak Spanish?"

197) An inmate was shown a copy of the Declaration of Independence and the date of 1776. He was amazed. "So this was the first time we got permission to light fireworks!"

In the final stage of learning the most magical moment is seeing success on an inmate's face. He has accomplished something he never thought possible. And it is then he realizes all those that helped him. All those that came down hard on him, not to punish him, but push him.

* * * * * * * * * * *

198) An inmate was asked to find the United States on a map. When he couldn't he was asked to find Mexico instead. "Where's that," he asked. The teacher replied it was south of the border. "What does south mean?"

199) An inmate asked what would hurt more, putting his hand directly into a fire or onto a heat vent. He was pretty sure it was the vent.

200) As it started to snow an inmate asked the teacher why that was. After the science went over his head the teacher simply resorted to telling him that he had forgotten to wish for it to sun. "See, I knew it," the inmate said. "That's why you're the teacher."